Brian Webb & Peyton Skipwith

Claud Lovat Fraser
DESIGN

Antique Collectors' Club

Design Series format by Brian Webb
Design: Claud Lovat Fraser © 2011 Brian Webb & Peyton Skipwith

World copyright reserved

ISBN 978-1-85149-663-1

British Library Cataloguing-in-Publication Data
A catalogue record for this book is available from the British Library.

Antique Collectors' Club
www.antiquecollectorsclub.com

Sandy Lane, Old Martlesham,
Woodbridge, Suffolk IP12 4SD, UK
Tel: 01394 389950 Fax: 01394 389999
Email: info@antique-acc.com
or
ACC Distribution,
6 West 18th Street, Suite 4B,
New York, NY 10011, USA
Tel: 212 645 1111 Fax: 212 989 3205
Email: sales@antiquecc.com

The cover design is reproduced from a Foxton cretonne fabric,
1920, and the decorated initials throughout the text are from
The Splendid Wayfaring, 1913
The Saracen's Head, opposite, was drawn for Lovat Fraser's
first exhibition of paintings, 1913, and used as a cover illustration
for The Book of Lovat, 1923
Page 23 Songsheet, Poetry Bookshop, 1921
Page 96 The Two Wizards, Flying Fame Chapbook, 1913

Published in England by the Antique Collectors' Club, Woodbridge, Suffolk
Designed by Webb & Webb Design Ltd, London
Printed and bound in China

LovatFraser

Design
Claud Lovat Fraser

ovat Fraser – universally known as Lovat – is one
of the great unsung heroes of 20th-century British
design. During his short life of just thirty-one
years, five of which were disrupted by the Great War,
he achieved an astonishing amount of work as a
draughtsman, watercolourist, caricaturist, publisher, illustrator
and designer of stage sets, toys and fabrics; he also designed silks
for Liberty, cretonnes for Foxton, advertising material for Eno's,
Mac Fisheries, Gurr Johns and J.&E. Atkinson, and book jackets for
Heinemann and Nelson, among others. His inimitable style
and psychedelic palette became the hallmark of both the Curwen
Press and the Poetry Bookshop, but he is best remembered today,
by those who are aware of him at all, for his poster, costume and
set designs for Nigel Playfair's 1920 production of *The Beggar's Opera*
at the Lyric Theatre, Hammersmith.

Lovat's life was undoubtedly shortened by his experiences in
the Great War, but, given his indifferent health, heart problems,
rheumatic fever and enormous girth, I suspect that even without
gas and shell-shock he was destined for a short life. A self-caricature
drawn around the time of his 20th birthday was reproduced on the
cover of the June 1910 issue of a Cambridge University magazine,
The Gownsman. Another self-caricature, drawn the following year, is
inscribed: 'All that was left of me, gallant six hundredweight'. They
both depict a dandified giant, seemingly in rude health, the second
showing him bursting out of tail suit, opera hat in one hand and
cane in the other. Three years later when he enrolled in the Officer
Training Corps at Catford he reverted once again in self-mockery
to Tennyson's 'Charge of the Light Brigade': 'Mine is not (now) to
reason why, mine is not (now) to make reply, mine is (now) to do
or die, gallant 1 1/2 hundredweight!'[1]

aldane Macfall in *The Book of Lovat*, published shortly after Lovat's death, touches on his friend's various ailments while fondly describing his character and figure: 'Romantically modern, Lovat yet loved and was of the dandified years of the eighteenth century – in taste, in vision, even in speech. His keen sense of humour early warned him that his bulk, his stature, his heavy form, would have fitted ill with the slender elegancies of the powdered wig, brocaded coat, and knee-breeches; and with laughing philosophy he compromised before his frank mirror between art and God's design of him by leaning towards the years of the Regency – the tight sleeve, the high velvet collar, the pantaloons, and the silk hat on the back of the head of a belated D'Orsay. He was the last of the dandies'.[2] Macfall also noted that: 'As though warned that he was early doomed, Lovat addressed himself to the career of art and letters feverishly; with restless energy that never flagged in his copious output.'[3] Two years after his return to London from the Western Front Lovat wrote in his diary: 'I have lived so long with Death as an opposite partner that I have of late rather ignored his existence.'[4] Whatever the causes – congenital weakness plus rheumatic fever, exacerbated by gas and shell-shock – his heart was dangerously weakened and could not stand the strain of an operation that he had to undergo in June 1921. He died at the Bevan Military Hospital Nursing Home in Sandgate, Kent. His glittering career cut short at its zenith.

Born in London on 15th May, 1890, into a comfortable middle-class family, Lovat Claud Fraser, as he was christened, was the son of Claud Fraser, partner in Clapham, Fitch, Cook & Co. – later, after 1911, Clapham, Fraser, Cook & Co. – a firm of solicitors with chambers in the heart of the City of London. His mother, Florence Margaret Walsh, was a lady of culture, eight years older than her husband, a skilled harpist – the love of which she attributed to her Celtic ancestry – and a talented watercolourist. The elder Lovat was a passionate devotee of the theatre, an enthusiasm he early passed on to his son, who, at the same time, inherited his mother's artistic flair. His schooling followed the convention for that of sons of successful professional men; after attending several preparatory schools, from the last of which, Mowden House, Brighton, he wrote to his parents in December 1903 requesting 'a little theatre for my Christmas present as I am writing a play', and commenting on the fact that he was not allowed to act as he was not a convenient size.[5] From there he went on to Charterhouse prior to a year's private coaching, before entering his father's firm in Devonshire Square, Bishopsgate, at the age of 18.

It soon became clear, whatever his father's hopes, that young Lovat's heart was not in the law, and during the two years he worked in the firm he filled his notebooks with sketches of the view from the office window, the passers-by in the square outside and quick caricatures of counsel and prisoners at West Ham Quarter Sessions. He had already developed the easy, fluent line that was to be the foundation on which he built his career, for he was to remain largely self-taught, apart from the lessons he had learnt from his mother and from C.W. Johnson, the art master at Charterhouse. Although Johnson had a distinct style, he never sought to impose it on others, and is remembered in the Charterhouse annals for encouraging the individuality of his students. Some of Lovat's sketches from this period were published in the school magazine, *The Greyfriar*.[6] His only formal training was a six-month spell at Westminster School of Art in 1911, where he studied etching with Sickert. By then he had drawn a number of covers for *The Gownsman*, at least one dust jacket for Heinemann, published a small book of caricatures and attracted the notice of Haldane Macfall, whose article, 'The Art of Lovat Fraser', appeared in *The Art Chronicle* that same year.

The caricatures that he drew with such apparent ease, modelling his style on Max Beerbohm and Ospovat, had their roots in his illustrations for *The Greyfriar*; the subjects he chose were either friends or people in the public arena, politicians and thespians – notably, Lord Rosebery and Arthur Balfour, H.G. Wells, Martin Harvey and Arthur Asche – and his outrageously simplified line drawing of Bernard Shaw appeared on the cover of a 1911 issue of *The Art Chronicle*. But caricature was only a youthful *jeu d'esprit*. Macfall described how Lovat loved to play at life, which he regarded as just a jolly game to be romped through in his spare time: 'His art was

First published as The Rapin in 1899, Toto, A Parisian Sketch was republished in 1910 by Heinemann. Henry De Vere Stacpoole, a ship's doctor for more than 40 years and an expert on South Pacific islands, was the author of the Blue Lagoon trilogy.

not a profession; it was the whole man, the essence and articulate expression of his life – the pencil or brush or pen never out of his industrious fingers [...] As though warned he was early doomed, Lovat addressed himself to the career of art and letters feverishly: with restless energy that never flagged in his copious output.'[7]

Lovat learned by example not just from Beerbohm and Ospovat but from the prints and drawings he studied in the second-hand bookshops in and around Charing Cross Road. Arthur Ransome, in *Bohemia in London*, written at that time, gives a vivid account of this bookish world. He describes the noise and bustle of the Charing Cross Road falling quiet for a few hundred yards as it drops 'all shout and merriment and boisterous efflorescence of business, and becomes as sedate and proper an old street as ever exposed books on open stalls to public fingers. [...] All about them are innumerable bound magazines, novels of Dickens, Scott, and Thackeray, novels of later times marked at half price, old sermons from sold vicarage libraries, old school grammars, and here and there the forgotten immortals of the nineties, essays published by Mr. John Lane, and poets with fantastic frontispieces. Against the window panes, behind the books, hang prints, Aubrey Beardsleys now, and designs by Housman and Nicholson, where once would Rowlandsons have hung, Bartolozzis, or perhaps an engraved portrait of Johnson or Goldsmith, done by Sir Joshua Reynolds, or perhaps again a selection of Amazing Beauties from the "Garland" or the "Keepsake" or the "Offering". [...] These shops are not the stalls that delighted Lamb and Gay before him. Those were farther east, some in Booksellers' Row, now cleared away by the improvements in the Strand, some in the neighbourhood of Covent Garden, some close by St Paul's, where in the alleys round about a few such shops may still be found.'[8]

Lovat's favourite haunt, as he lingered on errands from his father's chambers, was Dan Rider's Den, a little shop in St Martin's Court, where every available square inch was crammed with books and prints; here, the enthralled 20-year-old met not only the eponymous proprietor, but also Joseph Simpson and Haldane Macfall, who was destined to become successively patron, friend and biographer. It was this trio – artist, writer and connoisseur – that encouraged Lovat's father to allow him to renounce the law in favour of art, and it was then that he had his brief flirtation with Sickert's teaching at Westminster School of Art, and studied acquatint with Sylvia Gosse at Rowlandson House.

An important outcome of Lovat's meeting with Macfall was his introduction to the broadsides and chapbooks of the elder Joseph Crawhall – Northumbrian father of the Glasgow School painter – which he soon began to collect. In emulation of his new-found model, he abandoned drawing with a fine line in favour of the strong, purposeful, velvety-black strokes achieved through use of the reed pen. Although most of Lovat's work glows with colour, he was, like his friend Gordon Craig, essentially a black and white artist – but he was a black and white artist who had discovered colour at an early age and become intoxicated. His Charterhouse master, C.W. Johnson, was known by the boys as 'Purple Johnson', a nickname thought to be due to the fact that if a pupil's work was lacking in some way, he would say 'why don't you add some purple?' Lovat was never shy of adding purple, or magenta, or viridian or cobalt, to his bold pen and ink drawings; not as gentle washes but neat, virtually undiluted, so they sing like the early works of Vlaminck or Rouault. In 1913, E.V. Lucas, who had been recommended to him by James Pryde, commissioned a cover design for *Methuen's Annual*, which, when printed, drove Lovat to despair: 'so gross, so vile and so distorted a version of my cover sketch that I was almost mad with rage and grief – my original design was careful and staid in colour – this version of theirs was foul and vulgar.'[9] Lucas also bought a watercolour, *Solomon*, and christened Lovat 'The Vermilionaire'.

Lovat drifted into his professional career almost without noticing, swept up in his own enthusiasm as well as that of those around him. Within a short time he was producing illustrations for Macfall's *The Splendid Wayfaring*, making designs for the theatre and producing simple toys, inspired by those of the 18th and early 19th centuries, as well as by Gordon Craig's example. It was through *The Splendid Wayfaring* – or rather a related article – that both Macfall

The Smoker
The Splendid Wayfaring

Haldane Macfall's The Splendid Wayfaring was published by Simpkin
Marshall & Co. in 1913, with illustrations by Lovat, the author, Gordon
Craig and Gaudier-Brzeska. To enable Gaudier-Brzeska to draw and study
animals Fraser paid for the sculptor's season ticket to the London Zoo.

and Lovat met and befriended Gaudier-Brzeska, the impoverished French sculptor who was desperately trying to batter down the doors of prejudice and create a new three-dimensional visual language. Not surprisingly Lovat was in awe of Gaudier's drawings in which, through a few simple lines, he could define both form and character. He was among the first to be excited by Gaudier's talent, but soon drew away from him as Enid Bagnold recorded: 'Lovat, most indulgent of men, would never express dislike, but he could not waste time on Gaudier's burning, voluble, cascading talk, though he deeply respected his art.'[10]

acfall was proud of the precocious achievements of his young protégé, and the reader of his memorial volume is given the impression that he was responsible for guiding and influencing every aspect of Lovat's art, introducing him to Gaudier-Brzeska, Gordon Craig, Beerbohm Tree and the broadsides and chapbooks of the elder Crawhall. The article Macfall wrote on Crawhall's work could just as easily have been a description of Lovat's: 'He dips his hands into the stilted magnificence of the eighteenth century, gets a grip upon the elaborate etiquette and paste-buckled manners that held the time, and brings out in his deft fingers the discovered secret of the whole art of the chapbooks, with the bluff hint of his own deeper secret of artistry added to it. And his modern eyes – seeing the form of things more subtly than these Georgian folk saw it, seeing form with that deliberate grace that is the characteristic of our later-nineteenth century art, seeing it also with a full sense of its surface and body, and most of all its texture – he gives us the art of the chapbooks considerably glorified.'[11]

In January 1913 Lovat took a studio in Roland Gardens, Kensington, and it was here that he set up 'The Sign of Flying Fame', in partnership with Ralph Hodgson and Holbrook Jackson, to publish broadsheets and pamphlets in emulation of Gordon Craig's 'The Sign of the Rose'. Hodgson was to write the verse, Jackson the prose and Lovat provide the decoration. To this end each of the three partners subscribed five pounds; the printing was done by A.T. Stevens, a friend of Dan Rider's in St Martin's Lane. The joyousness of these little pocket-sized pamphlets attracted the attention of others, particularly Walter de la Mare and James Stephens, as well as Harold Monro, who had founded the Poetry Bookshop the previous year. However, not everyone responded in the same spirit. After reading one review, Lovat noted in his diary: 'Find nigh a whole page of denunciation and invective on "Flying Fame" – in the Athenaeum – none are spared save Walter de la Mare – Ralph Hodgson is "too outrageously simple" and I am God knows what kind of an imbecile muddler. We are "modishly affected" and make use of "clumsy compromise" and a whole page of it too. Well! Well! Well!'[12]

espite the ease with which Lovat poured out drawings and decorations, he remained highly self-critical, continually destroying drawings and watercolours with which he was not satisfied; of other people's work he tended to be less critical, though he could be quite tart in the privacy of his diary. In February 1914 he noted: 'Poor Macfall is very cut up by H[olbrook] J[ackson]'s luke warm notice of "The Splendid Wayfaring", which can't be helped. To tell the truth, I can't read it, although I half decorated it.'[13] A few weeks previously he had recorded: 'Demolish my old work. I tore up hundreds of watercolours. I have done better since. I keep about six out of two hundred or so.'[14] In *The Splendid Wayfaring* Lovat's rich black embellishments – chiefly head and tail-pieces and initial letters – jump off the page, in contrast to Macfall's own able but rather scratchy ink drawings indebted at many removes to Rembrandt. Lovat, Gordon Craig and Gaudier-Brzeska are all acknowledged on the title page of this ponderous tome, the frontispiece being a reproduction of an early watercolour by Gordon Craig, while Gaudier's contribution was restricted to a few line drawings of birds and animals. The book itself is pompously dedicated to the Crown Prince of Sweden.

During the second half of 1912, and the following year, the first chapbooks and broadsides were issued from the Flying Fame and Lovat, reaching his maturity, embarked seriously upon his career as a stage designer. Eight years had elapsed since he had requested a model theatre for Christmas, and during this time he had immersed himself in the study of English poetry, literature and drama. As his knowledge and appreciation increased he found himself irresistibly attracted to neglected masterpieces of the 18th century, especially Gay's *Beggar's Opera*. However, in the wake of Diaghilev's sensational 1912 season of the Russian Ballets (Ballet Russes), including Léon Bakst's revolutionary designs for the Polovtsian Dances from *Prince Igor* and *Scheherazade*, coupled with the popular success of Edward Knoblock's *Kismet* the previous year, audiences were agog for more of this exotic fare. Beerbohm Tree, always ready to oblige, was seriously considering staging Macfall's *The Three Students* to take advantage of this demand. Lovat, who already knew Tree, having designed his bookplate and illustrated his book of essays, *Thoughts and Afterthoughts*, set to work with alacrity designing costumes and sets. Tree, however, began to have second thoughts due, primarily, according to Macfall, to the fact that he no longer had a sufficiently youthful figure to assume the principal rôle. Whatever the truth, Lovat had already thrown himself into the project and had produced a number of designs before Tree and his company left for another of his regular tours of North America. Like *Kismet* and *Scheherazade*, *The Three Students* had an Eastern theme, and, from this time, Lovat regularly drew exotic figures, somewhat reminiscent of Frank Brangwyn's studies for *The Rubaiyat of Omar Khayyam*, adding odalisques and slaves to his well-developed repertoire of bewigged 18th-century characters.

Another dominating figure loomed large in Lovat's life at this time, the legendary Frank Harris, who, among other exploits, had hired a yacht and, in an interview at the Cadogan Hotel on that fateful evening of 5th April 1895, tried to persuade Oscar Wilde to flee the country before he could be arrested and tried. Harris had planted himself, cuckoo-like, in Dan's Den, and taken it over by sheer force of character, and had also assumed editorship of *Hearth & Home*, involving both Macfall and Lovat as contributors. This all came to an end with Harris's imprisonment in 1914. Harris was a charlatan, a self-invented character 'born in two different countries on three different dates and his name was not Frank Harris', as Lovat's friend and Harris's lover, Enid Bagnold, recorded.'[15]

Cover for Hearth & Home, 1913, *edited by Frank Harris.*

Despite the attraction of the exotic, Lovat remained at heart a very English figure. In his diary entry for 23rd February, 1914, he recorded his dream and his ambition: 'I should like to become one day the National artist of England such love do I bear her very hedges and ditches. Not a mere landscape painter or a depicter of rural "character" – heaven forbid, but one who should voice in his art the glory of Milton, Shakespeare and Shelley. What a wild ambition and at the present moment who am I but unproven Lovat Fraser?'[16]

His vision of 'Englishness' was generous and expansive, and his exuberance showed in everything he tackled from entire stage productions to papier-mâché ducks. His toy designs have a sophisticated innocence, though in the early days he was not happy with how they were executed: 'I go to the "Good Intent" to see my toys. Miss Darly sells poundsworths. She has sold £20 of them already, I have never had a penny nor wanted it, as the things have been atrociously carried out and look like designs made by a blind idiot'.[17] Later, as we will see, Ambrose Heal was attracted by them and commissioned Lovat to make prototypes from which the manufacturers could work.

All this creative activity, however, was interrupted by the outbreak of war. Lovat, despite his uncertain health and a severe attack of rheumatic fever earlier in the year, immediately volunteered and duly gained a commission in the Durham Light Infantry, with which he served at Ypres – but, early in 1916, after the battle of Loos, he was invalided home with shell-shock. Aware that at the Front he would not have access to an adequate supply of his favourite reed pens, he took pencils and watercolours so he could make sketches of people and buildings, and was delighted, later, when he heard that Sir Martin Conway had bought six for 'the National War Museum' (now the Imperial War Museum). These included *Donck's Brewery at Ypres* and two studies of *Costumes of the British Army in Flanders*. After several months of recuperation at the Red House, his father's country home in Buntingford, Hertfordshire – during which time, he illustrated two small booklets, *The Fairies' Farewell* and *Three Poems by Kenneth Hare* (both

For his 1915 Christmas card, drawn in Flanders, Lovat reverted to
steel pen and ink for his portrait of a survivor shelled out of her home.

printed by A.T. Stevens), and started on his large series of 'Notes on the Dress of His Majesty's First or Grenadier Regiment of Foot Guards' – he was posted to the War Office and assigned to the Intelligence Staff for propaganda work. By November he had been confirmed in his new job, and was working from the Army Records Office at Hounslow, Middlesex, in reasonable commuting distance of his old studio in Roland Gardens, South Kensington.

n February 1917, Lovat married the American singer Grace Crawford, and a new routine began: office in the morning, home in the afternoon, painting in the early evening and then to the theatre or opera, followed by dinner with friends. Grace became a partner in everything he did; in addition to singing, which she continued to perform professionally, she was a linguist and an adept and creative sempstress. 'Grace and I worked on the translation of Goldoni's "Liar". She doing the translation and I the dresses and general decor'[18] is a typical diary entry from this time. This fruitful collaboration was remarked on a couple of years later by E.O. Hoppé in his review of *As You Like It*: 'The costumes to the smallest detail were executed by the artist himself, who had only the assistance of his wife in this formidable task.'[19] He goes on to give a vivid firsthand account of the visual impact created by these costumes, which were made out of ordinary, unbleached holland, dyed by Lovat himself to achieve the precise colours he desired. Playfair also commented on Lovat's method of dying materials in the family bath, recording that on one occasion their baby daughter, who had been born the previous year, emerged from her evening tub 'with red and yellow streaks which lasted for weeks'.[20] In his review Hoppé noted: 'The materials are patterned in a delightful manner, and the character of their wearer is not infrequently expressed with quiet humour. The tight-fitting, parti-coloured tunics – small-waisted and with padded shoulders – worn in the Court circles are all in the most vivid colours: vermilion, emerald, lemon-yellow, crimson, cobalt; there are no half-shades. A pleasing sense of elasticity is created by toning down – as becomes their humbler station – the clothes worn by the figures in the forest scenes, but although colours are here subdued, the note of freshness and gaiety is not impaired.'[21]

During the last two years of the War, while occupied each day with his military duties, Lovat worked evenings and weekends on a wide range of studies and designs; he exhibited with the New English Art Club, worked on costumes and sets for John Drinkwater's Birmingham production of *The Liar*, toys for Heal's, textile designs for the Design and Industries Association's competition, which were later taken up by Foxton's, covers for Nelson's complete set of Dickens and designs for Nigel Playfair. His diary entry for 20th October, 1917, gives an idea of how driven he was at this time:

'Home early from the office and do a great deal of work.
> 1. A frontispiece for my father-in-law.
> 2. A scene for his play.
> 3. A scene for Peile's play (bad).
> 4. A scene for Playfair's revue.
> 5. Two costume designs for Peile's play.
> 6. A sketch for possible new picture.'

he collaboration with Playfair was to lead to Lovat's greatest triumph, *The Beggar's Opera*. On an impulse late in 1918 Playfair purchased the Lyric Theatre, Hammersmith, for the princely sum of two thousand and fifty pounds. Money which he could ill afford but for the help of Arnold Bennett, and so immediately set about trying to recoup some of the initial cost by commissioning A.A. Milne to write a children's review to replace the Lyric's traditional Christmas pantomime. Miraculously, *Make Believe – A Children's Review and Pantomime*, to give it its full title, was written, rehearsed and staged in three weeks, with scenery in the best fairy-book tradition, on which was superimposed, as Playfair recalled, 'several odd bits of cloth by Lovat Fraser'.[22] These 'bits of cloth' must have been among the earliest samples of his Foxton-produced cretonnes.

Nigel Playfair shared Lovat's passion for the neglected literature, drama and music of the 18th century, with the result that *Make Believe* was followed immediately by an English production of Pergolesi's *La Serva Padrona* (*The Maid Turned Mistress*). Playfair recorded

that this was the first production in which Lovat had been given
a free hand and, despite the fact that it only ran for two weeks,
persuaded him to try more 'eighteenth century stuff', even if the
public was not enthused. 'At that time', he wrote, 'the eighteenth
century was about as much out of fashion as it well could be: purity
of harmony could set on edge the teeth of the musical critic in a
way no cartwheel could. In literature we were all romantics, in the
seventeenth- and early nineteenth-century manner, or else realists
(which generally, in Drama, means romanticists turned sentimental
or sadist); and it was the thing to regard the eighteenth century as
a temporary chrysaliding of civilization – an attack of frost-bite
from which mankind did not recover till the genial rays of 1800
Romanticism.'[23] Once again it was a joint production with Grace
doing the translation and Lovat the sets and costumes.

Looking back, there is a curious dichotomy in the 20th century's
reassessment of the arts and literature of the 18th century. Playfair's
comments are backed up by those of Hugh Walpole who, while
writing *Rogue Herries* in 1928, noted: 'I must remember that no
one knows very much about the eighteenth century, or only a few
do. I can be venturous.'[24] Yet, at the same time, Joseph Duveen
was denuding many of Britain's grand houses, selling works by
18th-century artists to wealthy American collectors for previously
unheard-of prices.[25]

The Maid Turned Mistress was replaced at the Lyric in mid February
by John Drinkwater's *Abraham Lincoln*. This proved such a popular
success that Playfair had to postpone the staging of his new
production of *As You Like It*, on which Lovat had been working.
However news of his plans had filtered through the theatre
world, and he was invited to stage it that April as part of the
1919 Shakespearean Festival at Stratford-upon-Avon. Many in the
audience were shocked by Lovat's designs; the reviewer for *The
Morning Post* declared that the dresses were 'so daring and colouring
so extravagant in conception that they seem, to conservative minds
at any rate, out of all key with Shakespeare'.[26] Playfair recalled
one irate woman accosting Lovat in the street, shaking her fist
indignantly in his face, and demanding: 'Young man, how dare

The Forest of Arden, *Lovat's original design for Nigel Playfair's production of*
As You Like It *at the 1919 Shakespeare Festival at Statford-on-Avon. Grace Lovat*
Fraser noted that the pale buff leaves were originally emerald green, but that the inks
her husband used faded over the years.

you meddle with our Shakespeare!'[27] What Lovat had done, in fact, was to reject the Victorian – the Irving – tradition of Shakespearian costume, in favour of studying early missals contemporary with the supposed action of the play. To quote Playfair again, he 'copied these with such fidelity that he might have been quite certain the critics would accuse him of historic inaccuracy! […] Even his treatment of the forest scenery was not "cubist" as so many critics imagined; the looped curves by which he represented the foliage were copied exactly from a fourteenth-century missal, not from Picasso or Derain.'[28] A note by Grace attached to Lovat's sketch for this scene, *The Forest of Arden*, in the collection at Bryn Mawr College, throws an interesting light on his attitude and approach to design. In writing the note many years after the event, she recorded: 'The pale buff leaves were brilliant emerald green in reality – the colour has faded owing to Lovat's fondness for green ink, which was the precise colour he wanted. He always considered working drawings ephemeral and troubled only as to precision of colour not to its lasting quality.' The musical accompaniment for *As You Like It* was specially arranged from Elizabethan sources by Arthur Bliss, the young composer with whom Grace performed both at 139 Piccadilly, the London home of the Baroness d'Erlanger, and at the Wigmore Hall.

Lovat and Grace's daughter, Helen Lovat – known as 'Dorkler' – had been born on 29th April 1918, and the family moved to a more spacious home in Tregunter Road, where he continued, as usual, to work on a wide range of designs. The Flying Fame having been a casualty of war, he now linked up with Harold Monro and illustrated more than 20 rhyme sheets for the Poetry Bookshop, as well as writing and contributing verse under the pseudonym of Richard Honeywood. He joined the recently formed Design and Industries Association, enthusiastically sharing the ideals of its founders, most particularly Ambrose Heal, Joseph Thorp and Harold Curwen. It was in November 1917 that he first met Heal, who came to see him at his studio: 'A charming person. Public School and I think "Varsity"', he noted in his diary. 'Looks most uncommercial. A poet with a black felt hat. He knew all about me and enjoyed my work very much, he is seeing that some of my toy designs are taken up. He hints that my textile designs are

Sixteen Songs for Six Pence.

Pussy cat, pussy cat, where have you been?
I've been to London to see the Queen.
Pussy cat, pussy cat, what did you there?
I frightened a little mouse under the chair.

What's the news of the day,
Good neighbour, I pray?
They say the balloon
Has gone up to the moon.

Bell horses, bell horses,
What time of day?
One o'clock, two o'clock,
Three and away.

Arthur o'Bower has broken his band,
He comes roaring up the land.
King o' Scots with all his power,
Can't stop Arthur of the Bower.

There was an old woman
Lived under a hill;
And if she's not gone,
She is there still.

There was an old woman, and what
do you think?
She lived upon nothing but victuals
and drink.
But though victuals and drink formed
the whole of her diet,
The noisy old body would seldom
keep quiet.

The King of Spain,
with thrice ten thousand men,
Marched up the hill
and then marched down again.

Here am I, little
Jumping Joan;
When nobody's with me
I'm always alone.

Simple Simon went a fishing
For to catch a whale;
All the water he had got
Was in his mothers pail.

See-saw, Scaradown,
Which is the way to London Town?
One foot up and one foot down –
That is the way to London Town.

Jack be nimble,
Jack be quick,
Jack jump over
The candlestick.

A robin redbreast in a cage
Sets all heaven in a rage.

Jack Sprat could eat no fat;
His wife could eat no lean;
And so betwixt them both,
They licked the platter clean.

Three wise men of Gotham
Went to sea in a bowl,
If the bowl had been stronger
My song had been longer.

All of a row,
Bend the bow –
Shot at a pigeon
And killed a crow.

This is the House
Of the country mouse.

Designed and Decorated by C. Lovat Fraser and Published by The Poetry Bookshop, 35 Devonshire Street, Theobalds Road. London. W.C.1

amongst the six successful candidates in the "Design and Industries" Competition. I hope that it may be so. I should like to have my decorative work made use of. He likes my gloves and shoes and wants to get them taken up too.'[29] A couple of months later Heal introduced Lovat to Prudence Maufe, who ran his family store's Mansard Gallery, and they included a number of Lovat's toys in a selling exhibition later in the year alongside a loan display of 'Old Toys'. Lovat's designs were witty, simple and colourful – soldiers, model villages, animals, dolls' houses, Noah's arks, etc. – while many of the earlier historic toys on show came from his and Grace's own collection.

Having admired Lovat's bright, modern textile designs in the Design and Industries Association's competition, Ambrose Heal further encouraged him by introducing him to William Foxton, whom he brought to Lovat's studio in April 1918. Foxton used a number of Lovat's designs for a series of printed cottons, which they marketed during the next few years; these were largely non-figurative, geometric patterns, printed in bright colours, ideally suited to the post-war market and the early Jazz Age. Lovat used a similar non-figurative vocabulary for his pattern and cover papers and in his silk designs for Liberty, though for the latter he also produced several bright figurative patterns such as *Purple Cactus, Blue Houses* and the extraordinarily bold *Trireme*, with its vivacious and complex tracery of oars, banners and sails. During the autumn of 1919 he had a further exhibition at Heal's Mansard Gallery, showing this time a wide range of work, including watercolours, fabrics, model stage settings and posters. Albert Rutherston wrote the foreword to the catalogue.

Joseph Thorp, the gregarious 'Mr T' of *Punch*, was something of a fixer, who described his occupation, in 1924, on the register of founder members of the Double Crown Club, as 'Author, Publicist and Typographer'. His own small imprint – the Decoy Press – used the premises of the Curwen Press in Plaistow, East London, for which he acted as a self-appointed publicist, persuading Harold Curwen that, among other things, that his firm needed a trade sign. For this purpose he suggested they adopt the unicorn, and

Watercolour design for a costume fabric – for As You Like It – dyed in the family bathtub, from which the Fraser's daughter emerged 'with red and yellow streaks which lasted for weeks'.

immediately wrote the exuberant, promotional, public relations text, *Apropos the Unicorn*, with a pattern paper cover by Lovat.

Harold Curwen became so enthralled with Lovat's work that he bought a sketchbook containing more than 200 designs, some of which he used over the ensuing years to embellish various of his printing jobs, but, for more important projects, such as his own 1920 manifesto *Get the Spirit of Joy*, he commissioned fresh designs. Curwen also persuaded a number of his clients, including Mac Fisheries, the *Daily Herald*, Eno's, the Chelsea Book Club and the chemicals firm Boake Roberts, an East London neighbour, to commission work from Lovat. The Chelsea Book Club, in its modest way, was a publisher, and Lovat drew the decorations for an esoteric book of 12th-century French songs for them. Elsewhere I have related how Daniel O'Connor panicked, feeling that he had ordered insufficient copies from the Westminster Press of Charles Nodier's *The Luck of the Beanrows*, and so placed an urgent second order with Curwen for an additional thirty thousand, to meet his wildly overoptimistic estimate of the Christmas market.[30] Although not on quite the same dramatic scale, he repeated the process with a second Nodier book, *The Woodcutter's Dog*; the initial printing being by the De La More Press and the second by Curwen. For the cover of *The Luck of the Beanrows* Lovat created a geometric pattern of elongated, brightly coloured lozenges, similar to one of his earlier Foxton cretonnes.

Several other books illustrated by Lovat were printed at Plaistow: *The Lute of Love*, *A Long Spoon and the Devil* and *Poems from the Works of Charles Cotton*. The latter, a personal selection of works by this little-known 17th-century poet, was published in 1922 by the Poetry Bookshop, a year after Lovat's death. It bears an introductory note by Harold Monro that shows a less hectic, less driven aspect of Lovat's approach to work: 'Claud Lovat Fraser made his own selections from the *Poems of Charles Cotton*, transcribing them into a notebook and adding decorations from time to time between other work [...] Cotton's poems were a continual pleasure to him, and he was always trying to persuade his friends of their rare qualities. He was in sympathy with their period and their style.

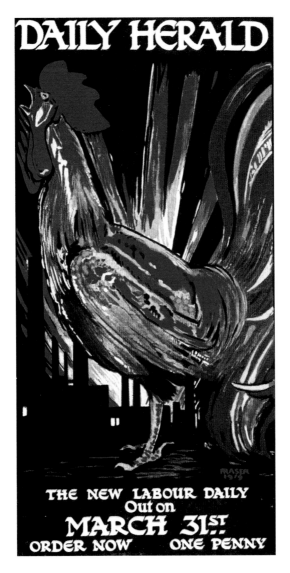

Original artwork, Heralding the dawn of a New Era; 10ft by 5ft (305cm by 183cm) lithographed poster announcing Francis Meynell's Daily Herald in 1919. Possibly hedging his bets, Meynell also printed McKnight Kauffer's vorticist woodcut Flight as a similarly sized poster.

His seventy-five drawings were done slowly and deliberately and with the greatest enjoyment. They represent him at his best as a book decorator and artist.'[31] It is hard to disagree with Monro, and the same claim could be made for a number of his other illustrated works, especially Walter de la Mare's *Peacock Pie*, published by Constable & Co. in 1924, though here his embellishments – to use one of Lovat's favourite words – had been made in 1912, and most of the poems published the following year.

Brilliant as Lovat was as an embellisher of books, broadsheets, and advertisements, as well as a designer of toys and textiles, and much as he enjoyed these activities and the outlet they gave him to exercise his impulse to decorate, the theatre was his most enduring passion. We have seen the 13-year-old schoolboy who wanted a model theatre because he was writing a play, the enthusiasm with which he put aside other work to produce designs for the abortive production of *The Three Students*, and his contribution to Playfair's quickly thrown together revue, *Make Believe*. But these were just curtain-raisers for his all-too-brief, but glorious, final years, during which time he designed Lord Dunsany's *If*, Tamara Karsavina's *Nursery Rhymes*, John Drinkwater's *Mary Stuart* and three further productions for Playfair: *The Maid Turned Mistress*, *As You Like It* and, most important of all, *The Beggar's Opera*.

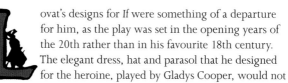ovat's designs for *If* were something of a departure for him, as the play was set in the opening years of the 20th rather than in his favourite 18th century. The elegant dress, hat and parasol that he designed for the heroine, played by Gladys Cooper, would not have looked out of place in one of Cecil Beaton's sets for *My Fair Lady* half a century later. Dunsany had always been intrigued by 'types', especially 'the beautiful lady who is utterly ruthless and the beautiful lady who talks with a common accent'.[32] Gladys Cooper in the rôle of Miralda Clement was the latter. The play, produced by Playfair at the Ambassadors Theatre ran for five months, and Dunsany was particularly impressed by Lovat's daring in setting Henry Ainley's scarlet uniform against Gladys Cooper's pink dress. Meanwhile, Tamara Karsavina was introduced to Lovat by the novelist, Hugh Walpole, whom she had met in Petrograd (Saint Petersburg) during

the war, and she commissioned costume designs from him for her ballet, *Nursery Rhymes*, as well as a poster, though the latter was never used. In her memoirs Karsavina paints an evocative vignette of Lovat sitting 'hunched in a basket chair in an attitude snug, but hardly suggestive of draughtsmanship, and at times using an odd implement – a nailbrush applied savagely on a finished design'.[33]

here is no doubt, however, that *The Beggar's Opera* was Lovat's finest achievement, and a fitting culmination to his years of devotion to the theatre in general and his obsession with 18th-century life, literature and costume in particular. John Gay's *The Beggar's Opera*, is one of the earliest examples of ballad opera, having been first performed in 1728. Two centuries on Playfair asked Arnold Bennett to make a suitable adaptation and, as he recalled, 'within a couple of days "The Beggar's Opera" had been analysed, dissected, and put together by him, and we had a version ready to be put to the test of rehearsal'. Frederic Austin was then 'locked up in a room' to complete his musical arrangement, while members of the cast were recruited from Sir Thomas Beecham's Opera Company.[34] Playfair describes how both he and Lovat overlooked the economics of mounting such a production, with the result that Lovat's initial designs had to be abandoned, although Playfair thought them perfection. 'But they wouldn't do, and I had to tell him. I did it very bluntly. It was the only way. I remember quite well even the words I used. I said: "Lovat, the whole damn thing has got to be done somehow in one scene, and you've got to produce that scene by tomorrow morning." I know his face went white, and I know his voice went husky, for he was a pretty tired man even then, but he only said: "All right." I think it was at one o'clock next morning that he rang me up and said: "I've found the way," and I knew by the sound of his voice that it would be all right indeed.'[35] It certainly was all right: *The Beggar's Opera* ran for 1,469 performances, closing in December 1925, only to be revived again the following year.

What Lovat had done was to devise for the scenery a single structure that, with only the slightest modifications, could be changed from interior to exterior and from elegant drawing room to grim prison

Unused poster design for Tamara Karsavina, a principal dancer of the
Imperial Russian Ballet before joining the Ballet Russes, who settled in
London and helped set up the Royal Ballet. Her biography, with decorations
by Lovat, was published by Cyril Beaumont in 1922.

– though, rather incongruously, the chandelier designed by Gordon Craig remained throughout. Although Lovat used more realistic sets and props than Craig, and delighted in the creation of visually gorgeous, but not elaborate, costumes, it is no surprise to learn that Craig, who accompanied him most days to rehearsals of *The Beggar's Opera*, resumed his own experiments with moving screens immediately on his return to Florence.

Death, so long Lovat's 'opposite partner', was now waiting in the wings. While enjoying a family holiday at Dymchurch in Kent, in the company of Paul and Margaret Nash and Athene Seyler – Rosalind in Playfair's *As You Like It* – and working on designs for Karsavina's *Jack in the Green*, he was admitted to hospital. An operation was deemed essential, but his heart could not stand it, and he died on 18th June 1921. He was buried in Layston churchyard (St Bartholomew's Church) close to the family home in Buntingford, and his name was inscribed on the base of the elegant war memorial cross, which he had designed for his favourite rural Hertfordshire retreat. Karsavina recorded that the design he sent to her on the eve of this fateful operation was probably his last drawing.

A few days later Playfair summed up his qualities and achievements in a short and moving tribute, which can not be bettered: 'Mud! That was what Lovat hated – it was the word he used as his severest form of condemnation – for pictures, plays, scenery, which offended him. He did not believe that the world was mud-coloured, nor that nature could be reflected on the stage in dun. […] I dread to think he is irreplaceable – it is so necessary that somebody should replace him. But the gifts that he must have! Draughtsmanship, a sense of colour, patience, humility, humour, diligence, honesty; a working knowledge of carpentry, architecture, of the costume of every century, lighting, grouping, movement, dancing, music; of the vast dramatic literature of this country, France, Italy, Spain and Germany; he must be able to write and lecture well and argue better, to receive rebuffs with a smile, to undo half that he has done at a moment's notice at the bidding of some economist... and all these he had, this boy who was always

tired and always laughing, always in pain and always trying
to make other people happy – who, at the age of 31 – with five
years of the War taken from his life – has left behind a collection
of several hundred drawings and paintings, of scene models,
of illustrated books, which will be forever one of the proudest
possessions of his country. *Requiescat in pace.* He may.'[36]

Peyton Skipwith

Gordon Craig On the Ponte Trinita, Florence, 1914. Craig's
A Living Theatre had been published in Florence a year earlier. The
title of the book Lovat has drawn under Craig's arm is 'All about me'

1. Macfall, H. (1923) *The Book of Lovat.* London: J. M. Dent & Sons, p. 124.

2. Ibid, p. 15.

3. Ibid, p. 17.

4. Lovat Fraser, C. (1918) Personal diary entry, 13 April 1918. Special Collections department, Mariam Coffin Canaday Library, Bryn Mawr College, Pennsylvania, USA.

5. Plumb, P. (1993) Introduction. In: Rogerson, I. (1993) *Claud Lovat Fraser: a catalogue of the illustrated books, broadsides, etc., accompanied by examples of the work of Albert Rutherston, Wyndham Payne, Elizabeth Mackinstry and Edward A. Wilson.* Manchester: Manchester Metropolitan University, p. vii.

6. I am grateful to Catherine Smith, archivist at the Charterhouse School Archive, for this information.

7. Macfall, op. cit., p. 17.

8. Ransome, A. (1907) *Bohemia in London.* London: Chapman & Hall, pp. 135–42.

9. Lovat Fraser, op. cit., 22 July 1913.

10. Bagnold, E. (1969) *Autobiography.* London: Heinemann, pp. 68–9.

11. Macfall, H. (1911) 'Old' Crawhall of Newcastle. In: *A History of Painting: the Modern Genius.* London: T. C. & E. C. Jack, p. 254.

12. Lovat Fraser, op. cit., 4 January 1914.

13. Ibid, 20 February 1914.

14. Ibid, 20 January 1914.

15. Bagnold, op. cit., p. 92.

16. Lovat Fraser, op. cit., 23 February 1914.

17. Ibid, 5 February 1914.

18. Ibid, 13 October 1917.

19. Hoppé, E. O. (1919) In: *The Studio,* Vol. LXXVII, July 1919, pp. 63–7.

20. Playfair, N. (1925) *Story of the Lyric Theatre, Hammersmith.* London: Chatto & Windus, p. 50.

21. Hoppé, op. cit.

22. Playfair, N. op. cit., p. 5.

23. Ibid, p. 31.

24. Quote. In: *Hart-Davis, R.* (1952) *Hugh Walpole: A Biography.* London: Macmillan, p. 288.

25. In 1921, Duveen sold Gainsborough's Blue Boy to Henry and Arabella Huntington for $620,000, while, 20 years previously, he had paid £14,050 for John Hoppner's Lady Louisa Manners, the highest price to date ever paid for a painting at a British auction.

26. Quote. In: Playfair, N. op. cit., p. 59.

27. Playfair, N. op. cit., p. 59

28. Playfair, N. op. cit., p. 49.

29. Lovat Fraser, op. cit., 21 November 1917.

30. Webb, B. & Skipwith, P. (2008) *DESIGN: Harold Curwen & Oliver Simon – Curwen Press.* Woodbridge: Antique Collectors' Club, p. 20.

31. Monro, H. (1922) Note. In: Monro, H. (Ed.) (1922) *Poems from the Works of Charles Cotton.* London: The Poetry Bookshop, p. 6.

32. Amory, M. (1972) *Lord Dunsany: A Biography.* London: Collins, p. 179.

33. Karsavina, T. (1948) *Theatre Street: The Reminiscences of Tamara Karsavina.* Revised and enlarged edition. London: Constable.

34. Playfair, N. op. cit., p. 92.

35. Playfair, N. op. cit., p. 98.

36. Playfair, N. op. cit., pp. 162–3.

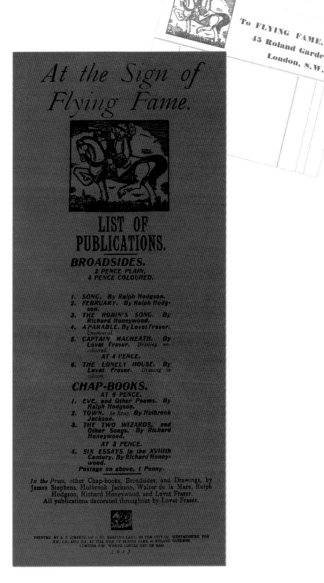

Lovat's Flying Fame device appeared on chapbooks, broadsides and stationery.

Town, printed in an edition of 600, and The Two Wizards, in an edition of 400, hand-coloured by Lovat, from the first series of Flying Fame chapbooks. Lovat wrote poetry under the pen name of Richard Honeywood.

Captain Macheath, The Beggar's Opera villain, makes his first
appearance as a Flying Fame print in 1913; 400 copies printed, price 2d.

Three Poems, by Kenneth Hare, and The Fairies' Farewell, by Richard Corbet, published for Everard Meynell each at sixpence, printed by A.T. Stevens of St Martins Lane, W.C. 1,000 of the little poem booklets were produced.

Commodore Trunnion.

Commodore Trunnion.

Sir Roger de Coverley.

Block proofs with colour experiments by Lovat for The Portraits of Three Old Gentlemen (My Uncle Toby not illustrated), 1916, for 50 hand-coloured sets of prints 'to be obtained from Everard Meynell Esq., the Serendipity Shop, 46 Museum Street, W.C.'. Everard Meynell was the son of the poet Alice Meynell and publisher Wilfred Meynell. Their youngest son Francis (later, Sir Francis Meynell) founded the Pelican Press in 1916 and the Nonesuch Press in 1922. He acquired McKnight Kauffer's Flight woodcut in 1919 to launch the Daily Herald.

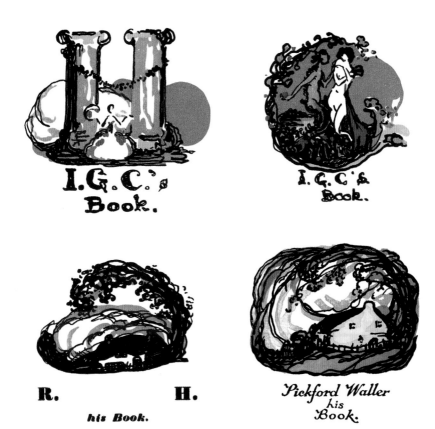

Sixty-three designs by Claud Lovat Fraser, *opposite. These were intended to decorate an edition of A.E. Housman's* A Shropshire Lad, *a collection of 63 poems. Harold Curwen bought Lovat's designs when Housman rejected them and they were published by the First Edition Club, in 1924, as a little book of drawings printed on hand-dyed Ingres paper and bound with a Lovat Curwen pattern paper.*

Bookplate designs, above, for Grace Lovat Fraser (née Grace Inez Crawford), Ralph Hodgson and Pickford Waller. Several more of Lovat's bookplates, including designs for Haldane Macfall, Desmond Coke and Herbert Beerbohm Tree, were published in the September 1921 issue of the Bookplate Magazine.

Aboo Ali
Act II.—The Three Students

Lovat worked on the design and sets for Haldane Macfall's 'Eastern' play, The Three Students, for several years on the understanding that the actor–manager Beerbohm Tree would produce the play. In the end, Tree rejected the play on the grounds of cost, that the public would not be attracted to the Eastern atmosphere (Kismet and Diaghilev's Scheherazade were, in 1911–12, all the rage), and that 'he no longer had the youthful figure to play the leading part'.

The Seat of Judgment
Act II.—The Three Students.

The Great Arras
Act III., Scene 2.—The Three Students

Hand-coloured Greetings for the American photographer, best known
for his portraits of Rupert Brooke and W.B. Yeats, who had established
a studio in London before the First World War. Schell became a well-
known modernist architectural photographer on his return to New York.

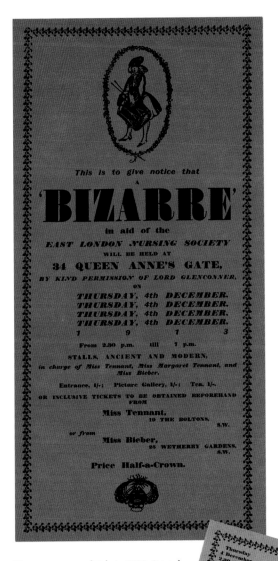

Bizarre, poster and tickets, 1913. Printed on 'Lovat' colour papers, orange, yellow, bright green and red, for a Charity Bazaar at the home of Lord Glenconner.

A
BOOK
of
SIMPLE TOYS
Designed by
C. LOVAT FRASER.
Traditional and
Otherwise.

1917.

LIGHT CAVALRY.

Gordon Craig had published his hand-coloured woodcuts in 1899 in his Book of Penny Toys, no doubt adding to Lovat's passion for simple toys, which only increased on the birth of his daughter. Ambrose Heal also commissioned designs and exhibited his collection.

You are invited to inspect a
LOAN COLLECTION OF
OLD TOYS
IN THE MANSARD GALLERY
From Nov. 22 until Christmas
and at the same time an Exhibition of
MODERN TOYS
of more than ordinary interest
which (unlike the old toys)
ARE FOR SALE

HEAL & SON LTD
195 Tottenham Court Rd.,
W. 1

1920.

A Jack-in-the-Box.

The Merry Lamb.

Cromer Mill.

Tumblers.

Bristol City.

Of 50 copies, No. 48

Bristol City lineblock print, 50 copies on thin tissue paper, 1916, and The
Lonely House, 400 copies printed in two colours on grey sugar paper, 1912.

No. 6.   Price 4 pence.
                                                          By post 5 pence.

THE LONELY HOUSE.

PRINTED BY A. T. STEVENS, OF 33 ST. MARTIN'S LANE, IN THE CITY OF WESTMINSTER, FOR R.H.,
L.F., AND H.J., AT THE SIGN OF FLYING FAME, 45 ROLAND GARDENS,
LONDON, S.W., WHERE COPIES MAY BE OBTAINED.

1 9 1 3.

The title page of The Dress of His Majesty's First or Grenadier Regiment of Foot Guards is supported by soldiers in 18th-century and First World War trench uniform. Pen and watercolour design for an unpublished book, 1915.

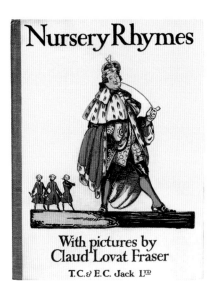

Nursery Rhymes was published in time for Christmas 1919, with 24 illustrations in colour and 64 decorations in black. The 'Piebald Horse and Rider' illustrated in the prospectus does not appear in the book.

TOM, Tom, the Piper's son,
   Stole a pig and away he run.
The pig was eat, and Tom was beat,
And Tom went roaring down the street.

CROSS PATCH,
   Draw the latch,
Sit by the fire and spin;
Take a cup
And drink it up,
      Then call your neighbours in.

AS little Jenny Wren
   Was sitting on the shed,
She waggled with her tail,
   And she nodded with her head.

She waggled with her tail,
   And she nodded with her head,
As little Jenny Wren
   Was sitting on the shed.

(This is the Shed.)

HERE am I, little
   Jumping Joan;
When nobody's with me
   I'm always alone.

WHAT'S the news of the day,
   Good neighbour, I pray?
They say the balloon
Has gone up to the moon.

NOW what do you think
   Of little Jack Jingle?
Before he was married
   He used to live single,
But after he married
   (To alter his life)
He left off living single,
   And lived with his wife.

JACK be nimble,
   Jack be quick,
Jack jump over
The candlestick.

THE cat was asleep by the
      side of the fire,
   Her mistress snored loud as
      a pig,
When Jack took the fiddle by
   Jenny's desire
And struck up a bit of a jig.

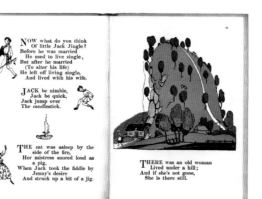

THERE was an old woman
   Lived under a hill;
And if she's not gone,
   She is there still.

Cinderella and the Slipper, *colour print.* The Decoy Prints were announced in
the first issue of Change, *the magazine (in fact, a little, hard-back book that ran to
only two editions) edited by Joseph Thorp and printed under the Decoy Press imprint
at Curwen Press in 1919.*

Lady on a Horse, *design for a cover, 1921. Owned by* Ambrose Heal, *whom Lovat had met through the Design and Industries Association (DIA), which was set up during First World War as a result of enthusiastic manufacturers seeing an exhibition in London of German products. Heal became a leading patron of Lovat's work.*

Box and bottle labels, c.1921, for Atkinsons' perfumes, from Lovat's scrapbook.
The Bath Soap label is a printer's proof, hand-coloured by Lovat for colour
reference. The Atkinson brothers introduced their lavender toiletries in 1910.
Although the company was sold in 1930, Lovat's designs were used for many years.

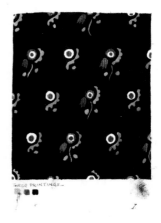

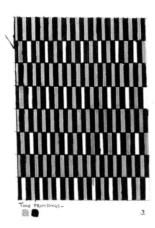

Paul Nash, in his introduction to A Specimen Book of Pattern Papers,
published by the Curwen Press in 1928, wrote: 'It appears that in 1920
Gordon Craig gave to the late Lovat Fraser one of those blank paper books with
the traditional patterned cover which are still produced in Florence. This seems
to have suggested to the ever resourceful "Lovat" the idea of making patterned
papers himself, and he proceeded to fill the pages with notes to that end.' Lovat's
designs were taken up by Harold Curwen and produced as large sheets for use as
book covers. Curwen went on to commission more artists, including Paul Nash,
Edward Bawden and Eric Ravilious, to add to 'Curwen Pattern Papers'.

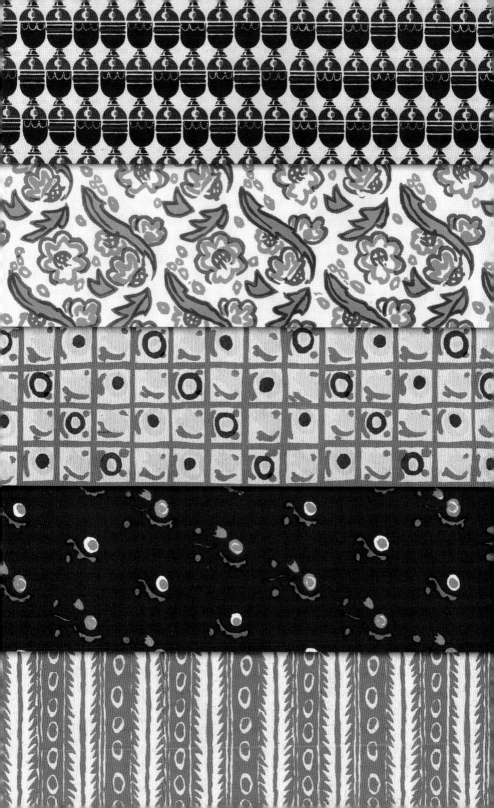

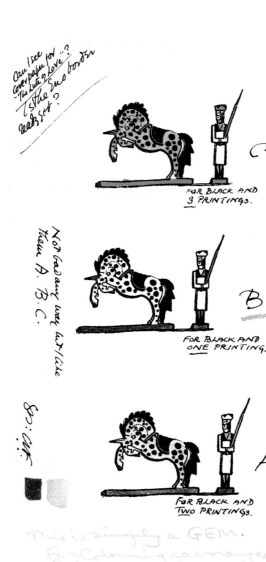

Lovat transformed the Curwen 'Unicorn' symbol from an heraldic device into a lighthearted children's toy.

The CUR
UNICOR
an intelligent a
venturous beas
is always tryin
strokes.

Your interest
quite as much, or
nearly as much,
your orders.

It's good fun to
good work, and it als
happens to be goo
business. Remember
the UNICORN of

The
CURWEN PRESS

HAROLD CURWEN
Plaistow, E.13

GET THE
SPIRIT OF JOY
INTO YOUR PRINTED THINGS

THE WORLD'S dead tired of drab dullness in Business Life.

GIVE your customers credit for a sense of Humour and some Understanding.

TAKE your courage in both hands and have your printing done

C H E E R I L Y !

I arrange & make
COURAGEOUS PRINTING
At the Curwen Press
Plaistow, London, E.13
Harold Curwen

Lovat put into pictures exactly Harold Curwen's desire to lift the spirits of his customers and bring gaiety to printing in the aftermath of the First World War. Curwen's 'careful printing' satisfied Lovat's critical eye.

GUILD OF SINGERS & PLAYERS

CONCERTS
AT THE STEINWAY HALL
at 8.15 p.m. on

WED. MAY 4

THURS. MAY 5
SIBYL CROPPER
ARTHUR SOMERVELL
The MARJORIE GUNN
QUARTET
Assisted by
Irina Meyrick and
Haydn P. Draper

The Programme will include
Quintet for Clarinet and Strings
(Arthur Somervell); Song Cycle
James Lee's Wife (A. Somervell);
Violin Solos (Max Reger); Quintet
in E minor for Piano and Strings
(Dohnányi)

Reserved and Numbered
3s. (including tax).
accompanied by a Stamped and Addressed
Free List.

A CHAMBER ORCHESTRAL CONCERT

At 139 PICCADILLY, W.1 *(by kind permission of the Baroness d'Erlanger)*, on WEDNESDAY, DEC. 15, at 9 p.m. precisely

GRACE CRAWFORD
(Mrs. C. LOVAT FRASER) &

ARTHUR BLISS

Assisted by THE PHILHARMONIC STRING QUARTETTE

Flute: A. FRANSELLA	Harp: GWENDOLEN MASON
Clarinet: C. DRAPER	Bass: C. HOBDAY
Bassoon: A. WILSON	Glockenspiel: } Side Drum: } J. H. PLOWMAN

PROGRAMME WILL INCLUDE BACH ARIAS WITH VIOLA OBB.
MOZART CONCERT ARIA WITH STRING ACCOMPANIMENT
AND A FIRST PERFORMANCE OF 'ROUT' FOR SOPRANO
VOICE AND ORCHESTRA BY ARTHUR BLISS

TICKETS TO BE OBTAINED FROM
THE BARONESS d'ERLANGER, 139 Piccadilly, W.1
Mrs. C. LOVAT FRASER, 23 Elm Park Gardens, S.W.10
ARTHUR BLISS, Esq., 21 Holland Park, W.11
PRICE OF TICKETS: ONE GUINEA, & HALF A GUINEA
(INCLUDING TAX)

A CHAMBER ORCHESTRAL CONCERT

At 139 PICCADILLY, W.1 *(by kind permission of the Baroness d'Erlanger)*, on WEDNESDAY, DEC. 15, at 9 p.m. precisely
GRACE CRAWFORD
(Mrs. C. LOVAT FRASER)
AND
ARTHUR BLISS
Assisted by THE PHILHARMONIC STRING QUARTETTE
Flute: A. FRANSELLA   Harp: KATHLEEN BARKWORTH
Clarinet: H. P. DRAPER   Bass: C. HOBDAY
Bassoon: A. WILSON   Glockenspiel: } Side Drum: } J. K. PLOWMAN
PROGRAMME WILL INCLUDE BACH ARIAS WITH VIOLA OBB.
MOZART CONCERT ARIA WITH STRING ACCOMPANIMENT
AND A FIRST PERFORMANCE OF 'ROUT' FOR SOPRANO
VOICE AND ORCHESTRA BY ARTHUR BLISS

TICKETS TO BE OBTAINED FROM
THE BARONESS d'ERLANGER, 139 Piccadilly, W.1
Mrs. C. LOVAT FRASER, 23 Elm Park Gardens, S.W.10
ARTHUR BLISS, Esq., 21 Holland Park, W.11
PRICE OF TICKETS: ONE GUINEA, & HALF A GUINEA

Shortly after their meeting in 1916,
Lovat married Grace Crawford, an
American singer. She went on to help
Lovat in the making of costumes and
translating plays, as well as continuing
her singing career.

Little Romances, a collection
of treasures. *Hand-coloured proof
and printed cover for Gurr, Johns
& Co. Insurance Valuers; booklet
printed by Curwen Press, 1921.*

The Blue Panther, *line block print,* 1921.

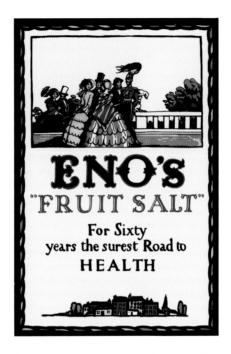

Eno's used Lovat's designs for a major advertising and poster
campaign in the early 1920s, and continuing after his death.

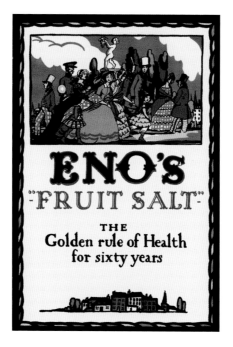

His work for Eno's was brought together in A Painting Book,
with biographical introduction by Joseph Thorp, printed at Curwen.

The Child as Artist

As I have said, obviously a painting book won't make the child an artist. It will merely, if used properly, provide a certain very simple and useful discipline in primitive craftsmanship.

The child should be in every way encouraged to observe objects about the house and in the streets, and invited to put them down from memory. And this exercise may be varied by the preferred and in itself most salutary exercise of drawings 'out of the head,' which need have no relation to life as grown-ups see it, or to the correct principles of anatomy or perspective.

It is too easily forgotten that Art has really essentially little to do with the 'correct representation' of things. That is the camera's job. The artist tries to express an idea, a vision, of his own. Clearly the artist whose drawings are here represented saw common things in an uncommon way and made beauty out of them, freely and almost at haphazard.

Art is of the soul first, of the hand next, of the rule and compass (not at all, and many a labouring craftsman may have something to say and his sincerity enable him to say it, however haltingly, while another man, competent and slick may put down something which is correct if you measure it, but dead if you look into it.

All of which is a little too solemn for a trivial occasion. All that (I suppose) I want to convey is that no parent or teacher should take the responsibility of discouraging positively or by indifference, the budding aspirations of the child to express himself as paper with pencil, brush, or crayon.

Putting on the Colour

For water-colour give the child a small pudding basin of clean water which will not easily upset; a few small saucers or an old large plate will do for a palette. Encourage the children's work by giving them more colours and more convenient apparatus (e.g. a china palette with divisions) as they improve. But, I repeat, give good colours and good brushes however few to start with.

The colour to be applied should be mixed up thin enough to flow readily from the brush. The paint should be laid carefully to the outline, not slopped over it, and the tint should be even, not streaky, and transparent, not 'muddy' (which comes from too thick paint). The child should experiment in the mixing of the few colours and learning the proportions required to fix other colours.

When using the coloured pencils the colour should not be merely scribbled in, but carefully built up,

The Beggar's Opera *opened at the Lyric Theatre, Hammersmith, on 5th June 1920 and instantly secured Lovat Fraser's reputation. The cardboard model was made to Lovat's design as a first anniversary souvenir in 1921. The 'drop curtain' with* Prospect of Newgate *rises to the setting of Act 1 of the play.*

S O N G S *from*

THE BEGGAR'S OPERA

MACHEATH AND POLLY.

AIR.—Over the Hills and far away

Were I laid on Greenland's Coast,
And in my Arms embrac'd my Lass ;
Warm amidst eternal Frost,
Too soon the Half Year's Night would pass.

POLLY.

Were I sold on Indian Soil,
Soon as the burning Day was clos'd,
I could mock the sultry Toil
When on my Charmer's Breast repos'd.

Macheath. And I would love you all the Day,
Polly.   Every Night would kiss and play,
Macheath. If with me you'd fondly stray
Polly.   Over the Hills and far away.

AIR.—Bonny Dundee.

MACHEATH.

The Charge is prepar'd ; the Lawyers are met,
The Judges all rang'd (a terrible Show !)
I go, undismay'd.——For Death is a Debt,
A Debt on Demand.——So take what I owe.
Then farewell, my Love——Dear Charmers, adieu.
Contented I die——'Tis the better for you,
Here ends all Disputes the rest of our Lives.
For this way at once I please all my Wives.

AIR.—Have you heard of a frolicksome Ditty, &c.

MACHEATH.

How happy could I be with either,
Were t'other dear Charmer away !
But while you thus teaze me together,
To neither a Word will I say ;
But tol de rol, etc.

THE POETRY BOOKSHOP, 35 DEVONSHIRE STREET, W.C.1   [No. 1]

S O N G S *from*

THE BEGGAR'S OPERA

POLLY.

AIR.—Grim King of the Ghosts, &c.

Can Love be control'd by Advice ?
Will Cupid our Mothers obey ?
Though my Heart were as frozen as Ice,
At his Flame 'twould have melted away.

When he kist me so closely he prest,
'Twas so sweet that I must have comply'd :
So I thought it both safest and best
To marry, for fear you should chide.

AIR.—Thomas, I cannot, &c.

I, like a Ship in Storms, was tost ;
Yet afraid to put in to Land ;
For seiz'd in the Port the Vessel's lost,
Whose Treasure is contreband.
The Waves are laid,
My Duty's paid.
O Joy beyond Expression !
Thus, safe a-shore,
I ask no more,
My All is in my Possession.

AIR.—Now ponder well, ye Parents dear.

O ponder well ! be not severe ;
So save a wretched Wife !
For on the Rope that hangs my Dear
Depends poor Polly's Life.

THE POETRY BOOKSHOP, 35 DEVONSHIRE STREET W.C.1   [No. 2]

The success of The Beggar's Opera generated a mass of souvenirs:
song sheets, portraits of the original cast, prints and books.

THE

BEGGAR'S OPERA

By Mr. GAY

A New Edition of the Text of the Play, containing
all the Original Airs in Facsimile. Illustrated
with eight Colour Plates of the Characters
and Scenes, and Black and White Decorations by C. LOVAT FRASER.

Royal 8vo.   15s. net.

Also a Large Paper Edition on English hand-made
paper, limited to 350 numbered copies.
£3 3s. net.

WILLIAM HEINEMANN

20 & 21, BEDFORD STREET, LONDON, W.C.2

King Lear. Unused design for the set of Act 1, Scene 1.

Lovat drew dust jacket designs for 18 volumes of the Nelson's New Dickens series for Thomas Nelson & Sons.

Nicholas Nickleby

3/6 net

Nelson

Little Dorrit

3/6 net

Nelson

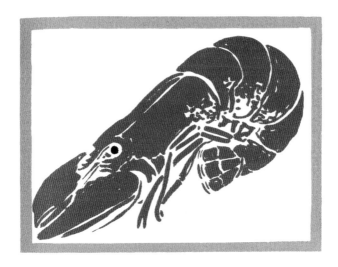

'Crabs and Lobsters are Now at their Best'

'Mac Fisheries know the best fish obtainable today'

'Oysters are in season Now'

'New Mackerel fresh and fine'

'Pointers', gummed labels for attaching to Mac Fisheries posters advertising fresh stocks of fish.

RHYME SHEET [Second Series]

STAFFORDSHIRE

O, hips and haws are scarlet,
  And all my time's my own,
So I will go to Yarlet
  Or maybe into Stone;
For Autumn is the season
  And golden is the morn,
And clearly shows the reason
  That ever I was born.

In robes of red and yellow
  The tall trees are arrayed;
Then come forth every fellow,
  And come forth every maid:
Come Jonathan and Charlotte,
  Come Timothy and Joan,
And take a walk to Yarlet,
  Or maybe into Stone.

Poem by Oliver Davies
Decorations by C. Lovat Fraser

The Poetry Bookshop
35 Devonshire Street
W.C.1

(No. 22)

Curwen Press, Plaistow, E.13

RHYME SHEET [Second Series]

THE ROBIN'S SONG

God bless the field and bless the furrow,
Stream and branch and rabbit burrow,
Hill and stone and flower and tree,
From Bristol Town to Wetherby—
Bless the sun and bless the sleet,
Bless the lane and bless the street,
Bless the night and bless the day,
From Somerset and all the way
To the meadows of Cathay;
Bless the minnow, bless the whale,
Bless the rainbow and the hail,
Bless the nest and bless the leaf,
Bless the righteous and the thief,
Bless the wing and bless the fin,
Bless the air I travel in,
Bless the mill and bless the mouse,
Bless the miller's bricken house,
Bless the earth and bless the sea,
God bless you and God bless me!

Poem by Richard Honeywood
Decorations by C. Lovat Fraser

The Poetry Bookshop
35 Devonshire Street
W.C.1

(No. 21)

Curwen Press, Plaistow, E.13

Harold Monro, poet and publisher of the Chapbook, owned the Poetry
Bookshop. His illustrated Rhyme Sheets included poems by John Drinkwater,
Charles Cotton, Ralph Hodgson, Eleanor Farjeon and Lovat himself.

At the same time as designing pattern papers for Curwen, and as an extension to the designs for theatre costumes, Lovat was designing textiles. His designs for Foxton were successful in a DIA organised competition. (The diamond design, bottom left, became the cover pattern of The Luck of the Bean Rows in 1921.)

CRETONNE.
Designed by C. Lovat Fraser.
For Wm. Foxton.
1920.

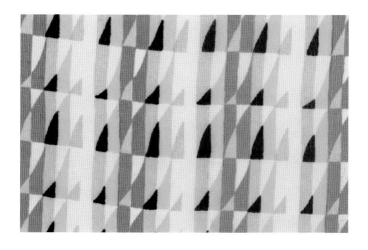

Printed silks for Liberty & Co. c.1920.

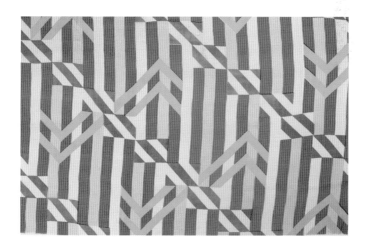

Blue House, Trireme and Purple Cactus;
printed silks for Liberty & Co., c.1920.

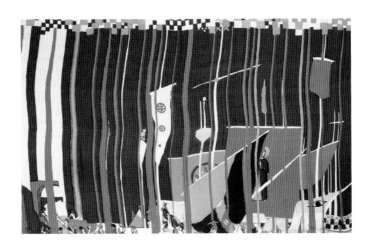

The Tempest, *design for the set of Act 2, Scene 1.*

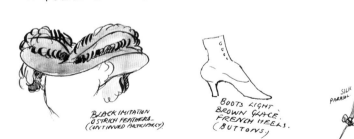

Sketches for Gladys Cooper's costume in Lord Dunsany's play If,
produced by Nigel Playfair at the Ambassadors Theatre, 1920.

FABRIC ON WIRE
FRAME

THIS IS A VERY ROUGH
SKETCH.

Jack in the Green for Karsavina, 1921. Possibly Lovat's last drawing.

SIMPLICITY

ACTION

SPEED

ACCURACY

A GREAT STEP FORWARD

'An Amazing machine which will affect every business house from this day'

A Great Step Forward, 'The New Comptometer'. Illustrations for a 16-page booklet promoting a revolutionary adding machine, and also used as an 8-page advertisement insert in System magazine, February 1921. The comptometer was invented by Dorr E. Felt in Chicago and introduced in 1887. 'The New Comptometer' could 'add, subtract, multiply and divide'.

GOLDONI'S COMEDY

THE LIAR

TRANSLATED FROM THE ORIGINAL BY
GRACE LOVAT FRASER

WITH A PREFATORY NOTE BY
EDWARD GORDON CRAIG

AND FOUR ILLUSTRATIONS BY
C. LOVAT FRASER

The Liar, *a Venetian comedy by Carlo Goldoni, published by Selwyn & Blount, 1922.*

The Bearer of Fruit, originally drawn as a limited edition print, coloured by hand, was used as the cover for The Art Chronicle in December 1922.

GRACE LOVAT FRASER
THEATRICAL COSTUMES FANCY DRESSES
AMUSING MODERN CLOTHES
13 ELM PARK GARDENS, CHELSEA, S.W.10
Tel. Kensington 7209

11 TREGUNTER ROAD
THE BOLTONS · S·W·10
LONDON

An Account of money due to C. Lovat Fraser.
from
for

A. WILME COLLIER LTD
8th Avenue Works, Manor Park, London, E.12
"DEX" PASTE & SPRAY PASTE
GLUAK VEGETABLE GLUE
Representative
MR. RICHARD SYMONDS
Telephone: ILFORD 751

23 ELM PARK GARDENS
CHELSEA S.W.10
LONDON
Tel. Kens. 7209

An Account of money due to C. Lovat Fras
from
for

The FIRST

NELL STEWART
ONE CLARGES STREET, PICCADILLY, W.1
Telephone: Grosvenor 1213

Sells
Fruit and Flowers
Wreaths and Bouquets

Attends to
Palms, Conservatories,
Window Boxes & Floral Decorations

Sold to

£ s. d.

With C. Lovat Fraser's
Compliments

DECOY PRESS
PLAISTOW · LONDON · E·13

Mrs C. Fraser,
13 Cranswell Gardens,
S.W.5.

YOU ARE INVITED
to come to HEALS and to
bring Children to see the
TOY GARDEN
Christmas 1923
196 Tottenham Court Road

With
Mr. Christopher
Millard's
Compliments
& thanks

AN EX
SEL
HOUS
TH
Chosen for
Strength, Pl
Practical Desig
penny Catalogu
ful and practica
ADMISSION
Arranged by the Desig
Association of 8 Queen S
October 11th to Dec
WHITECHAPEL ART G
Nearest Tube: Aldgate East, Dis
Hours 11 to 9. Open on S

The Bungalow
8 Abercorn Place
London, N.W.8
HAMPSTEAD 3359

Some of the hundreds of decorations drawn by Lovat...

…and used for the Curwen Press and other printers.

Safety First. Calendar, rough design (above) and printed, illustrated (opposite), issued by London Underground Railways and the DIA. Frank Pick, the managing director of the London Underground Group, was an early member of the DIA, and commissioned several poster decorations from Lovat. The calendar, 12 cards hung by a string, ran from September 1921 to August 1922.

It's your Safety. Seek it.

Save lives not Minutes.

Short cuts are Wrong cuts.

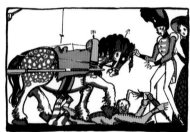

A Short Cut, a Quick End.

A Clear Crossing means a Safe Crossing.

Care avoids wheels and woes.

Caution is the Parent of Safety.
(N.B. This Design is Emblematical.)

Always have time to be careful.

40 Prints only

No. 13.

Vase, 1921.

Acknowledgements

In the Mariam Coffin Canaday Library at Bryn Mawr College, Pennsylvania, there exists the most remarkable archive of the work of Claud Lovat Fraser. While researching this book, and talking to people about Lovat Fraser, I have been asked time and again how the archive of this unduly neglected British artist came to be at Bryn Mawr. The answer is simple and touching. In 1924, a Philadelphian book collector, Seymour Adelman, was reading an edition of Ralph Hodgson's poems published under the Sign of the Flying Fame and embellished by Lovat Fraser. Fired by this initial introduction, Mr Adelman actively sought for Lovat Fraser material. His quest led to an enduring friendship with Lovat's widow, Grace, and the acquisition of many of the papers and drawings that remained in her possession. Along the way, he had also managed to acquire the collections of two of Lovat's earliest admirers, Haldane Macfall and Christopher Millard, thus creating the unique archive that is now at Bryn Mawr. I am deeply indebted to its guardians, Eric Pumroy and Barbara Ward Grubb, for their unfailing help and kindness in giving me access to this material. Eric Pumroy is not only Director of Library Collections at Bryn Mawr College, but enjoys the extra privilege of being the Seymour Adelman Head of Special Collections. Without his encouragement, and the Antique Collectors' Club's financial support in helping defray the expenses of my October 2009 visit, my appreciation of Lovat's life, and the richness of material here illustrated, would have been greatly depleted. Brian Webb joins me in thanking Tom Phillips, Ian Rogerson, Alison Plumb, Catherine Smith, Anne Harding, Robin Cox, Patrick Rylands, the staff of the London Library, and private collectors.

FINIS